Chingford As It Was

A Selection of Photographs

© Chingford Historical Society
Friday Hill House, Simmons Lane, London, E.4
Bulletin No. 10
1977

ISBN 0 904514 10 2

Front Cover : Kings Head Hill c.1900.

Back Cover : An advertisement of 1906.

CHINGFORD AS IT WAS

This book of photographs from the Society's collection attempts to give a glimpse of Chingford before 1920. Unlike Walthamstow, which by 1911 had largely been built over, and had acquired a population of over 124,000, Chingford was still at that time largely rural, with a population of just over 8,000.

The railway had been extended to Chingford from Walthamstow in 1873 and again in 1878 to the present terminus, and after that date there was a gradual development of the Chingford Rise Estate on the Pole Hill side of Station Road. Elsewhere it was still fields—Mount Echo, Gomme's, Pimp Hall, Larks Hall, Normanshire, Cherrydown, Little Friday Hill, Low Hall—the names of the farms are preserved in road names now.

In White's **Directory of Essex** for 1863, Chingford is described as "an irregularly built but pleasing rural village . . . and contains 1174 inhabitants, and 2459 acres of land, including a large tract of open common land, and about 200 acres of wood on the western side of Epping Forest. The surface in many places rises high, and commands varied and extensive prospects". Revd. Robert Boothby Heathcote of Friday Hill House was rector, John Pearson was the National School master, George Bartrip was carrier to London on Mondays and Fridays (he was also parish clerk), there were two bakers, two blacksmiths, three shoemakers, three carpenters, two tailors, two wheelwrights, four grocers (including George Bartrip again and George Banks), and nineteen farmers. The local inns were the Bull & Crown, the Fountain, the King's Head and the Prince Albert.

Kelly's **Directory of Essex** for 1912 has indications of the coming rapid urban development for it refers to the village being lit by the Gas Light & Coke Co., water being supplied by the Metropolitan Water Board, to being governed by an Urban District Council, to the Congregational and Wesleyan churches, the Walthamstow Sanatorium (now Chingford Hospital), the Chingford Mount cemetery, the police station, and the New Road schools. There are still farmers, though, like James Soper at Low Hall, who also had a shop in Station Road, James Wood at Chingford Hatch, Charles Jessop at Larks Farm, and Charles Edsall at Gomme's. Other names still familiar to Chingford residents are—John Banham, greengrocer; Alfred Blaxland, grocer; William Edmonds, cycle agent; Edmund Law, butcher; Arthur Methven, fried fish shop, Frank Randall, baker; William Tanner, chemist; Frank Toe, hairdresser; John Warren, bootmaker, and Walter Westcott, laundry.

Canon Alfred Russell was rector of Chingford from 1878 to 1919 and he recorded major local events in his parish magazine. In the April 1904 issue he referred to the forthcoming tramline to be built from Walthamstow to the Prince Albert, and to the offer of an acre of land by Mr. F. G. Sinclair for a new church and vicarage (now St. Edmund's) "for the expected new increase in housing". Only six years previously the Essex Otterhounds had met near the Old Church and hunted along the River Lea! The war delayed but did not stop the spread of suburbia to Chingford.

W.G.S.T.

The Green Man in Old Church Road 1859-60.

The Green Man fifty years later.

The Old Bull & Crown in the 1890's. It stood behind the present building which was erected in 1899.

The Fountain Inn, Low Street, now Sewardstone Road, c.1898.

The smithy in Station Road which stood opposite the present library, c.1885.

George Bartrip's coal depot which stood where the Roman Catholic Church is now.

Jessup's wheelwright shop, Chingford Hatch.

Hatch Lane looking west towards the Prince of Wales, c.1910.

Calver & Skeets' grocery shop which stood on the corner of Chingford Mount Road and Bateman Road, c.1912.

Chase Lane, the Chingford end, 1913.

Flanders Weir which was on the River Lea due west of the Old Church. The site is now under the Girling reservoir.

The entrance to Larks Wood by Inks Green Farm house which was demolished a few years ago.

Some Chingford worthies!

Chingford's first football team photographed in Bull Field, next to the Bull & Crown.

Canon A. F. Russell, Rector of
Chingford 1878-1919.

George Bartrip, the last Parish
Clerk.

Mrs. Leach, formerly owner of the
Bull & Crown.

Mr. Weston, formerly proprietor
of the Bull & Crown.

Queen Elizabeth's Hunting Lodge more than a century ago.

The old horse pond at the top of Kings Head Hill in the 1890's. In 1896 it was filled in. The man is filling the water spraying cart from a stand pipe.

The Old Church, Bank Holiday, 1900.

The New Church on the Green c.1870. The architect was Lewis Vulliamy and it was built in 1844.

Chingford Hall. The site is now the factory area in Hall Lane.

Friday Hill House, also designed by Lewis Vulliamy in 1839, was the home of the Boothby Heathcotes until 1940.

Spencer's Farm, Low Street, now Sewardstone Road.

Larks Hall Farm, c.1910. It has recently been saved from demolition for conversion into homes for single people.

Grandfather in the hayfields where Richmond Road is now.

Pimp Hall with house, dovecote, and barn.

The Royal Forest Hotel before the disastrous fire of 1912.

The Avenue, now part of Rangers Road near Bury Road c.1900. Note the horse brakes and Royal Forest Hotel in background.

Chingford Station shortly after it was opened.

Station Road c.1910.

Chingford Mount Cemetery at the turn of the century. It was opened in 1884.

Looking up Chingford Mount with the cemetery entrance on the right. It was laid out on the site of Caroline House.

Walthamstow U.D.C. electric tram at the Prince Albert Terminus. The tram line
was opened in July 1905.

Chingford Road between Hampton and Sinclair Roads c.1910. Some of these houses
have recently been demolished.

Chingford Fire Brigade during the first world war, outside the old fire station on the corner of Pretoria Road.

Chingford's first motor fire appliance c.1920.

In 1911 an aeroplane made a forced landing in a field behind the Old Church. Next day it took off and flew back to Hendon.

The motor delivery van from Nash's laundry at The Green.

This view is taken from by the Old Church looking north, so that Chingford Avenue now goes away to the right and Leadale Avenue goes where the path leads to the left down to Flanders Weir.

Looking up Kings Head Hill from the Low Street junction c.1910.